Original title:
Starlight on Christmas Snow

Author: Robert Ashford
ISBN HARDBACK: 978-9916-94-114-0
ISBN PAPERBACK: 978-9916-94-115-7

Radiance Over the Silent Ground

A glowing thing just hit my nose,
I thought it was a snow-filled rose.
But there it sat, a snowman grinned,
With buttons made of peppermints pinned.

The flakes fell down like fluffy pies,
Landing softly, a sweet surprise.
I slipped and slid, oh what a show,
My face now packed with frosty dough!

Winter's Ethereal Glow

The moon was bright, a disco ball,
Reflecting light on sheets so tall.
A squirrel skated without a care,
On a pond with flair, it’s quite a scare!

The icicles hung like fancy bling,
Draped over houses while carolers sing.
The only sound is giggles loud,
As snowmen dance beneath the cloud.

Luminous Frosted Dreams

The sky is dressed in glimmering quirks,
While giggling snowflakes do their work.
They tickle noses and tangle hair,
In a winter waltz, a lively affair!

Hot cocoa spills on my mittens' seam,
As I laugh aloud, it's like a dream.
Marshmallows float with a cheerful cheer,
In this snowy world, the fun is clear!

Twinkling Spirits in the Chill

A Christmas tree with laughter bright,
Full of ornaments and pure delight.
My cat’s beneath, in a festive trance,
While the dog tries to join in the dance!

Snowflakes tumble like playful clowns,
While bundled kids roll upside downs.
Winter wonderlands bring silly glee,
As we all stomp through the frosty spree!

Fragments of Heaven upon Earthly White

Tiny twinkles dance with glee,
While snowmen wobble, not like me!
Elves in socks, they take a slide,
As snowflakes tickle, can't we hide?

Hot cocoa spills, no one is dry,
Snowball fights with a gentle cry.
Mom's mittens lost to the breeze,
Yet laughter echoes through the trees.

A Symphony of Light in Winter's Silence

Giggles burst like popcorn in air,
While reindeer plots to steal a pear.
Frosty whispers through chilly nights,
As marshmallows fly in snowy flights.

Santa's sleigh stuck in a drift,
Elves debating the best gift.
With tinsel tangled in the race,
They trip and tumble, 'Oh! What grace!'

Glistening Nightfalls on Crystal Clouds

The moon's a giant, grinning wide,
While penguins slide, oh what a ride!
Snowflakes wearing hats of fluff,
Singing songs, but not enough.

Chilly noses coming to play,
As shadows stretch and skiers sway.
A snowman’s smile starts to melt,
With every joke that we've all spelt.

Rays of Joy upon the Snowy Canvas

Silly hats and bright red boots,
Laughter echoes, playful hoots.
Snowball chaos, a friendly war,
Who knew snow could spark such lore?

Hot nog spills on frosty toes,
While neighbors peek through wintry do's.
The lights begin to twinkle bright,
As squirrels dance beneath the night.

Dazzling Crystals under a Starry Vault

Sparkling flakes in a frosty dance,
They tickle my nose, not giving a chance.
Snowmen wobble, hats all askew,
Their carrot noses might just say boo!

Sleds zooming down with jubilant squeals,
I take a tumble—oh, how it feels!
With each wild crash, laughter takes flight,
As jolly snowballs are thrown left and right.

Glorious Reflections on Silent Landscapes

Mirrors of snow reflect moonlit grins,
As I chase my dog—he's off to win!
Pawprints zigzag like a playful maze,
While I slip and slide in a comic haze.

Frosty breath forming clouds in the air,
I look like a dragon—can’t help but stare!
Hot cocoa spills, marshmallows afloat,
As I giggle and choke on my cinnamon coat.

Winter's Radiance beneath the Celestial Dome

Ice crystals shimmering all around,
My boots squeak loudly, what a silly sound!
A snowball battle breaks out in delight,
And somehow, I’m caught—sorry, not bright!

Trees wear white like a festive gown,
While I spiral down, spinning around.
With each goofy fall, joy fills the night,
As I lie in the snow, chuckling outright.

Enchanted Frost on Starry Evenings

Under the glow of a chilly breeze,
I stack up snowballs like seasonal cheese.
A snowflake lands atop my hot tea,
And I laugh as it makes a splash, oh me!

With mittens on hand, we twirl and glide,
Yet somehow I trip—do I need a guide?
Chasing bright lights in this snowy terrain,
Falling again, it’s a comedy campaign!

Luminescent Nightfall

The moon slipped on a banana peel,
As snowflakes giggled with a squeal.
Santa’s sleigh got stuck in the frost,
Rudolph laughed, ‘At least I'm not lost!’

Elves danced in boots that were way too big,
Twinkle toes took a charming jig.
Hot cocoa spilled in a frosty sprint,
While marshmallows plotted, having a tint.

Velvet Snow and Twilight's Kiss

Frosty the Snowman lost his hat,
He’s now a pancake, how about that?
Countless snowmen laugh with glee,
Making angels in the snow with tea!

Chilly cheeks and noses so red,
Wishing for cookies, and maybe some bread.
Hot cider warms in a dancing mug,
While gingerbread men pull a quick hug.

Enchanted Dewdrops of Midnight

The cat chased shadows on sparkling ground,
While fairies whispered, ‘Let’s fool around!’
A snowball fight broke out, oh what a sight,
With snowy birds joining in the night!

Sledding downhill, we’re going too fast,
Zooming past trees, this fun cannot last!
We spill down the hill, laughing with pride,
The sleigh got hijacked, watch us slide!

Echoes of Light in the Quiet Dark

Laughter echoed through the chilly light,
As snowmen claimed the holiday night.
Under twinkling stars, we came to play,
Making wishes, hoping for ballet!

The cocoa’s hot, but the marshmallows flee,
Each one convinced it's a game of tag, you see!
Dancing in circles, they swirl and sway,
While kids chase laughter, without delay.

A Paean to Light in Snowy Solitude

In the night, the snowflakes dance,
A glimmering chance for prancing ants.
With cocoa spills and mugs askew,
The snowmen cheer with googly eyes too.

The cat in boots attempts to slide,
On frosty hills, what a crazy ride!
He tumbles down, the snowballs fly,
As laughter echoes through the night sky.

One tree in a hat, oh so shy,
Winks at the moon, while the squirrels try.
They throw snowballs, oh what a blast,
Until the winter pelt wins at last.

Carrots and twigs, all mismatched glee,
With frosty breath, come join with me.
We'll toast to the chill, and laugh so loud,
In the shiny glow of the wintery crowd.

Glittering Dreams Caught in Wintry Shadows

Frosty flakes tickle our noses wide,
We chuckle as snowmen start to slide.
One cheeky fellow, with a snazzy tie,
Looks quite dapper, oh my oh my!

The reindeer prance in mismatched shoes,
While Santa's sleigh sneezes with the blues.
Each jingle bell plays a silly tune,
As they dance around, under the moon.

A snowball fight breaks out in style,
With snowflakes sweetening every smile.
Winter's a riot, with giggles to spare,
Decorated snowflakes dance in the air.

The chimney's puffing out billowy smoke,
As hot cocoa’s swirling in every poke.
Raise your cup, let’s toast to the cheer,
And laugh 'bout the snow that won’t disappear!

Celestial Tones in a Draped Wonderland

The stars above, like sprinkles bright,
Make every snowflake a twinkling sight.
With frosty pants and bumbles galore,
Each slip on the ice brings laughter and more.

The snow's a blanket, all fluffy and white,
Tempting the kids to launch into flight.
In sleds and toboggans, they zoom down the hill,
Shouting with glee, a wintertime thrill.

A pair of mittens, mismatched and worn,
Finds a friend on a chilly morn.
They frolic and tumble, what a grand spree,
Chasing each other with snow-laden glee.

The sprightly lights hang low from the trees,
Making the shadows dance with the breeze.
Laugh, sing, shout on this merry day,
In this holiday fun, let's sway and play!

Whispers of Frosted Gleam

Twinkle toes on icy ground,
Elves are dancing all around.
Snowflakes whisper, giggles loud,
Winter's joke, we are all proud.

Sleds are zooming, laughter flies,
Hot cocoa spills; oh what a surprise!
A reindeer slips, falls with flair,
Snowman grins, without a care.

Frosty hats, a crooked grin,
Snowball fights, everyone's in.
Giggles echo through the night,
Jokes take flight, what a sight!

Winter wonder, silly cheer,
Frosty pranks, we persevere.
Boundless fun, with snow galore,
Let’s go play, who could ask for more?

Celestial Tinsel Aglow

Frosty lights from rooftops drip,
Santa’s stuck, can’t make the trip!
Tinsel tangled, oh what a mess,
Christmas cheer, we still confess.

Chilly penguins, skating fast,
Running circles, love to blast.
Cookies missing, crumbs on the floor,
Gingerbread men plotting war!

Snowflakes tumble, swirling round,
Fallen angels on the ground.
Marshmellow fluff as snowballs fly,
Laughter bounces off the sky.

Bells are ringing, laughter flows,
Funky hats in pink and prose.
With silly antics, we take a bow,
Winter’s show, let’s join somehow!

Moonlit Drifts of December

Shiny boots, a fashion quest,
Sleds are flying, who’s the best?
Snowy faces, cheeks that glow,
Oops! Another slippery throw!

Frosty noses, rosy blush,
Racing squirrels in a rush.
Snowman giggles, carrot nose,
Dancing lumbar, oh what a pose!

Hotcakes flipping, syrup spills,
Snowball battles, all the thrills.
Icicles hanging, pranks unpack,
Elves in trucks, vroom-vroom, whack!

Laughter echoing, bright and bold,
Winter's tales, endlessly told.
So let's embrace this snowy dance,
With silly antics, take a chance!

Glittering Silence

Silvery flakes in the air,
Making snow angels without a care.
Frosty windows, chill and fun,
Santa’s reindeer? Out for a run!

Giggles muffled under layers,
Snowball launches; watch out, players!
Gingerbread pants, oh what a sight,
Cakes in tutus, dancing light.

Twinkling tricks and playful schemes,
We’ll toast to presents, thoughts, and dreams.
With every chuckle, winter sings,
Joyful hearts, what laughter brings!

Snowstorms tease, a funny fight,
Chasing shadows in the night.
So here we are, hearts aglow,
Winter’s giggle beneath the snow!

Night's Jewel on Purest White

Twinkling gems in the night,
Dancing on the chilly ground.
Snowmen wearing hats too tight,
Laughter echoing all around.

Frosty friends with carrot noses,
Struggling to keep their balance.
Sliding down on snowy poses,
Winter's joyful, silly malice.

Magical Glimmers in the Winter Breath

Bubbles of laughter fill the air,
As snowflakes play hide and seek.
Snowball fights without a care,
And hot cocoa brings a cheeky peek.

Reindeer prancing in the frost,
Wearing scarves that look so bright.
Finding mittens that we've lost,
All while singing silly fright.

Illuminated Paths of Serenity

Guided by light beneath the moon,
Luminaries of the night.
Sleds go zooming, oh what a tune,
While parents sip cocoa in delight.

Wandering souls in jolly guise,
Stumbling over snowman feet.
Laughter echoes, glowing eyes,
While frosty air competes with heat.

Frosted Wishes and Wandering Souls

Wishes whispered on chilly breeze,
Tickling noses, causing glee.
Snowflakes trickle from the trees,
As kids shout, "Look! A snowman pee!"

Frosted hats and boots that squeak,
Slides turned into giant hills.
Chasing squirrels with squeals so freak,
Each snowy venture brings us thrills.

Moonlit Frost and Glistening Hush

Under the moon's chilly beams,
Snowmen plot with frosty dreams.
They huddle close, whispering plans,
While penguins dance with winter fans.

Icicles hang like crooked teeth,
Sleigh bells jingle beneath their wreath.
Hot cocoa spills on wooly mitts,
As snowflakes tumble doing flips.

Snowball fights with overgrown aims,
Launching dreams in snowy games.
Yet doggos chase and stealthily leap,
While giggles fly and laughter creeps.

So raise a glass of snowman cheer,
For winter fun, let's not shed a tear!
Let's toast to silliness and delight,
As frosty capers shine so bright.

Radiant Serenades of Winter's Eve

Socks on feet, a comical sight,
Sliding around, it's pure delight.
Puddle swirls where snow once laid,
As laughter bubbles, joy displayed.

Chubby cheeks with rosy glows,
Fluffy hats where giggles flow.
Winter boots that squeak and squeal,
Life’s a snowball, oh, what a deal!

Birds in hats made from old tins,
Singing songs where the fun begins.
They tease the cats who plot below,
While raucous fun steals the show.

Beneath the stars, the antics rise,
With twinkling eyes and silly sighs.
Let’s jingle all with merry glee,
As winter’s charm dances carefree.

Dances of Light Upon Frozen Ground

Squirrels skitter with frosty flair,
Chasing shadows of snowflakes in air.
They twirl and leap, a ballet act,
While frosty breezes play the soundtrack.

Mittens lost in the swirling white,
Cats embark on their daring flight.
With leaps and bounds, they foolishly chase,
Gliding past with a fluffy grace.

Cocoa explosions, oh, what a mess,
As marshmallows join in a fluff fest.
Snowball targets? Cats just can’t see,
They pounce and miss, then flee with glee.

Under the stars, the giggles bloom,
As winter evenings fill the room.
So dance along, let the nonsense grow,
In the shining laughter of the snow.

Ethereal Sparks in the Winter's Chill

Gingerbread men on a snowy run,
Sprinting fast for frosty fun!
With candy buttons as silly charms,
They giggle loud as they flee from farms.

Fluffy foxes in snowshoe strife,
Wobble through their whimsical life.
Paws are tangled; tails twist and fly,
As winter whispers a jovial sigh.

Sleds crash down with a hilarious bump,
While giggles echo in every thump.
Through crisp nights, the laughter swells,
With moonlit stories, that slip and fell.

So gather 'round the crackling glow,
Where winter fun steals the show.
With merriment wrapped in these cold nights,
Let’s dance with joy beneath the lights.

Celestial Dances on Frozen Glimmers

Twinkling stars with snowflakes race,
They tumble down in a cosmic chase.
Snowmen wobble, their noses askew,
While squirrels in mittens plot to break through.

Laughter echoes, a frosty delight,
As penguins slide, oh what a sight!
A snowball fight erupts with a cheer,
Hilarious faces, we can’t help but jeer.

Frosty the monster dances with glee,
Every chilly step is nature's spree.
Snowflakes chuckle, they shimmy so bright,
In this winter wonder, all feels just right.

So grab your cocoa, let the fun flow,
As we whirl and twirl through the soft glow.
With giggles and wiggles, the night we’ll adore,
In this frozen arena, forever we'll soar.

Shining Hopes in a Frosty Wonderland

The moon grins down on a chilly scene,
While fluffy white blankets cover the green.
Sleds zoom by, with laughter galore,
And snowflakes whisper, 'Who wants to explore?'

Gingerbread houses sprout like weeds,
With candy cane fences and sugar plum seeds.
Elves on roller skates zoom right by,
Spreading cheer as they giggle and fly.

A reindeer sneezes, a dance in his leap,
While icicles dangle, their company deep.
Children kick snow like they're in a game,
Each little snowball has its own name.

So join the parade, let your spirit ignite,
In this frosty realm where pure joy takes flight.
With laughter and fun, let the wonders bestow,
A night filled with warmth despite the cold's glow.

A Tincture of Twilight on Soft White

With dusk settles softly, the lights start to gleam,
As snowflakes dance in a wintery dream.
A cat in a sweater prances around,
While kids build a fort, laughing loud with no sound.

A snowball whizzes past Santa's big hat,
'Twas aimed at the snowman, but hit the old cat!
With the jingle of bells, and mischief in play,
We yell, 'It's a Christmas! Hooray, hooray!'

Puppies in boots chase shadows around,
As the sparkly glitters fall soft to the ground.
The cocoa is spilled, but, oh what a thrill,
To share silly stories and wintertime chill.

As night drapes its cape in the soft snowy glow,
We dance and we prance, with our fears laid low.
Laughter and warmth fill the frosty expanse,
In this whimsical moment, we all have a chance.

Night's Embrace on a Blanketed Glow

The stars like sprinkles on white frosting steep,
While we giggle and frolic, our secrets to keep.
At winter's own ball, the owls take the lead,
As trees dressed in snow shake their branches with speed.

Silly snowballs fly with expert finesse,
Hitting unsuspecting adults in their dress.
A dog in a scarf leaps high into the air,
Spreading pure joy like it just doesn't care!

The moon plays hide and seek behind fluffy clouds,
As jolly nonsense ensues in the crowds.
Each footstep crunching in rhythmic delight,
Turns snow angels into a glorious sight.

With rosy-cheeked friends and the cool evening breeze,
We bask in the magic of winter’s freeze.
Whimsical wonders, mischief’s own glow,
In the heart of the night, let the laughter flow.

A Celebration of Light in Winter's Cradle

Snowflakes fall like confetti,
Sprinkled on our frosty ground.
Elves slide by on slippery pants,
Laughter echoes all around.

Hot cocoa spills in merry cheer,
Marshmallows dance like tiny stars.
Frosty noses laugh and jeer,
As snowmen shout, "We're the cars!"

Icicles twinkle, a shiny treat,
Carrots lost in snowman hats.
Who needs a sleigh? Let's hit the street,
With sleds that roar and playful spats!

So gather 'round, let's raise a cheer,
For winter's charms and festive fun.
With every fall, let joy draw near,
As sunlight fades, our night’s begun.

Celestial Shimmers on Immaculate Peace

The moon is winking from the trees,
As we stack presents way too high.
Bows can fly like winter breeze,
Landing on dogs who run nearby.

A snowball fight turns into chaos,
One launch misses, but still gives grace.
We laugh so hard, it feels like play-doh,
As snow drifts cover every face.

Singing tunes that warp and bend,
Off-key notes, yet spirits soar.
Furry friends, the perfect blend,
As they chase down a squirrel galore!

So here we dance under frost and light,
With hiccups from laughs that melt the chill.
In twinkling hours of frosty night,
Memories carved, the heart they fill.

The Quiet Glow of Frosty Remembrance

A quiet night, but who would know?
Santa's sleigh is stuck in the snow.
Rudolph sneezes—a funny sight,
With a glowing nose that lights the night.

Gifts are tangled like a puzzle wide,
Tinsel flies, full of festive pride.
Cats chase shadows, and oh, what fun!
As we recall that we've just begun.

Grandma's roast—too burnt to bite,
We laugh and munch on fruitcake bright.
Whispers float like bubbles in air,
As snowflakes twirl without a care.

So let us gather, hearts and food,
In this season, our spirits renewed.
With giggles, hugs, and memories clear,
Each frosty glow is a heart's warm cheer.

Chasing Light in a Snowbound Haven

Snowmen wobble with carrot noses,
As giggles echo through the trees.
Fluffy friends leave snowy poses,
Searching for warmth with playful ease.

Sleds go whoosh, down hills they glide,
Yelling "Catch me!" with frosty breath.
Snowballs fly; it's a wild ride,
Laughter sings, defying death!

Lights above blink as if to tease,
While choirs croon their festive tunes.
With cocoa sips and playful freeze,
We dance beneath the laughing moons.

So gather 'round, let spirits bloom,
As winter hugs us in its arms.
Each twinkle brings a spark of gloom,
Yet joy shines bright—oh, what charms!

Glint of the Night Sky on Snowy Dreams.

In winter's chill, we dance and prance,
The flakes fall down, a festive chance.
We slip and slide, a comical scene,
As snowmen grin, all jolly and keen.

What’s this I see? A cocoa spill,
My mittens soaked, yet I feel the thrill.
With marshmallows bobbing like little boats,
I laugh so hard, I lose my coats!

The moon winks bright, a jolly fellow,
While snowflakes twirl in a merry yellow.
Sledding down hills, we scream with glee,
Gnomes throwing snowballs—fun for free!

So here we are, with cheeks aglow,
Under the shimmer of a frosty show.
For when the night brings its snowy charm,
Life’s a grand jest, with winter’s farm!

Whispers of Frosty Luminescence

A jingle bell rang, my hat flew away,
Frosty whispers kept me at play.
With snowflakes falling on kids and hounds,
We built a sled, just to fall down!

Under the glow of bright, twinkling lights,
We dance like penguins in silly fights.
The robin's mailbox has lost its flair,
But everyone's laughing, we don't care!

A reindeer passed by, wearing a bow,
I offered it snacks—brought my pet crow!
With giggles and grins, we made quite a mess,
Wintertime joy, oh what a happiness!

Snowflakes gather on noses, oh dear,
But laughter erupts, that's the holiday cheer.
With snow angels flapping their glittery wings,
We toast to the nights that funny luck brings!

Twinkling Dreams in Winter's Embrace

Under a sky of glimmering white,
The snowflakes dance in sheer delight.
I tripped on ice and fell on my bum,
But up I sprang, all giggles and fun!

The frost is nippy, my cheeks burn red,
But laughter fills the air as we spread.
We join in a chorus of snowball fights,
And giggled away into frosty nights!

An elf on a shelf lost his candy cane,
In a blink, I ate it, oh, what a shame!
With chocolate on my face, I couldn’t look proud,
But winter’s antics make laughter loud.

So here’s to the snow, the fun and the cheer,
For in every cold, there's warmth in here.
With silly songs, and friendships so bright,
We’ll twinkle and laugh through this frosty night!

Celestial Glimmers on Silent Nights

A silent night, or so they say,
But then came a cat, in pjs, hooray!
She jumped in the snow, all fluffy and bold,
Rolling like dough, oh what a sight to behold!

We packed up the flakes, chuckling with glee,
Creating a snowman who spilled my tea!
With carrot nose tilted, all goofy and round,
He blinked at us—oh, laughter abound!

The stars above twinkle, like fireflies bright,
While we build a fort, ready for the fight.
Our snowball arsenal is bursting with fun,
Let’s launch them now—oh, what have we done?

So join the frolic under the moon's glow,
Where giggles and grins make winter's show.
With every cold sip, and marshmallow raise,
We laugh till we drop in this snowy maze!

Frosty Candles in the Moonbeam

Frosty candles dance and sway,
Chasing shadows far away.
Snowflakes giggle in the air,
Tickling noses, causing flair.

With each flicker, secrets drop,
Like a snowman's silly hop.
Joyful laughter, warm and loud,
Even the cold can't feel too proud.

Pine trees wear their gleaming hats,
While squirrels wear their chubby mats.
Up the path, we'll make a run,
Chasing snowballs, oh what fun!

Underneath the moon's embrace,
We dance the night with silly grace.
Frosty candles light our way,
Merry mischief, come out and play!

Shimmering Goods of a Winter Hearth

By the fire, we share a tale,
Of reindeer antics and a snail.
Stockings hung with sweets and glee,
Who knew Rudolph liked to ski?

The cookies stacked up way too high,
Did Santa need a jet to fly?
Gifts wrapped snug with ribbons tight,
But why's the cat hiding tonight?

Hot cocoa spills, oh such a mess,
Marshmallow snowmen claim distress.
Do they melt or do they float?
In our mugs, they like to gloat!

A winter hearth with laughter bright,
Funny games chase away the night.
With shimmering goodies all around,
Who needs more? We’ve laughter found!

Frostbitten Radiance

Frostbitten joy, a sprightly glow,
Snowmen grinning from below.
The dog slips on the icy patch,
All our giggles seem to match.

Twinkling lights upon the trees,
Who knew branches swayed with ease?
Falling icicles play a tune,
The cats all sing beneath the moon!

Sleds go zooming, but wait for me!
There goes a snowball aimed at Lee!
Frosty breath and cheeks so red,
Magic lives in cozy beds.

Laughter brightens every lane,
With each tumble, there's no pain.
Frostbitten fun and joyful grit,
In our hearts, the joy will fit!

Crystal Shards in the Deep

Crystal shards beneath our feet,
Jingle bells and frostbitten heat.
We skate in circles, cheers abound,
Watch out for that snowball mound!

Slipping here and sliding there,
Whispers of fun fill the air.
A snowball fight breaks out in glee,
Who's winning? Not quite sure, you see!

Shivering giggles, cozy cheer,
Tell me, does that squirrel wear a beard?
Racing snowflakes, laughter flies,
As we chase the winter skies.

So here's to joy in chilly air,
With crystal magic everywhere.
Frosted fun will never cease,
In winter wonderland, we find peace!

Shimmering Crystal under a Velvet Sky

Under twinkling lights, we prance,
With dancing snowflakes, we take a chance.
Snowmen wave, their arms like sticks,
While reindeer slip on holiday tricks.

Hot cocoa spills, a marshmallow fight,
We giggle and tumble, what a sight!
Penguins march, with their wobbly flair,
As snowballs fly through the frosty air.

Frosty nose and cheeks that glow,
A snow angel mimics my goofy flow.
Laughter echoes in the chilly night,
While everything sparkles, oh so bright!

With twinkling stars in the deep, deep blue,
We catch our breath with silly views.
Under the shimmering, cozy blend,
This merry chaos will never end!

Luminous Reflections on a Silver Blanket

A blanket laid across the park,
With snowflakes falling, bright and stark.
We build a fort with a royal decree,
The king of snowmen is calling me!

Giggling children in fluffy attire,
Tell tales of a cat who caught fire!
Sledding down hills, the speed’s absurd,
But landing flat's the funniest word!

Cocoa clinks in mismatched mugs,
While puppies chase the winter bugs.
We toast to fun, with sticky hands,
Planning snowball fights, in these snowy lands.

As we dive into the marshmallow fluff,
Let’s make some magic, it’s never tough.
With laughter bright, and cheer not slow,
Come dance with me in the silver glow!

Frosted Echoes of Nighttime Wonder

The moon peeks through, a cheeky grin,
While snowmen try to join in the din.
A cat on a sleigh, with a tip of its hat,
Rides by singing 'I'm too cool for that!'

Pine trees wear coats of frosted white,
Squirrels are making a raucous plight.
Snowflakes tickle our noses with glee,
As we slip and slide, oh can't you see?

We attempt to catch snowflakes on tongues,
While carols play out of key in songs.
Chilly fingers and toes that freeze,
Yet we giggle loudly, with such carefree ease!

Magic happens when the laughter's loud,
As icicles form upon cheeks, so proud.
Under this wonder, we skip and cheer,
It's a frosty party, come join right here!

Celestial Wonders upon the Snowy Stillness

Stars above are twinkling bright,
A snowy scene that's pure delight.
Bunnies hop in coats too snug,
In this chilly world, they give a shrug!

Sledges flip, as we race and play,
The snowman grins, it's a livelier day.
Hats that fly and scarves that whirl,
In this snowy chaos, boys and girls.

Mittens lost, but who even cares?
Pine cones tossed show our quirky airs.
As we leap through powders of pristine bliss,
A roll in the snow? Oh, don't you miss?

With frosty laughter and cheeks aglow,
We'll cherish these moments, don't you know?
Beneath the wonders that make us smile,
We celebrate winter with our wacky style!

Glistening Echoes of the Night

The snowflakes dance, what a sight,
They wiggle and giggle, sheer delight.
A penguin slips, oh what a fall,
Santa laughs, can't help at all.

The moon, it winks, what a tease,
While Rudolph frets, his nose does freeze.
Frosty’s hat has taken flight,
Chasing shadows, what a night!

The carolers sing out of tune,
A reindeer plays a kazoo, quite a boon.
The snowmen argue, hats askew,
All while sipping on cocoa too!

With mismatched socks and cheerful cheer,
They tell tall tales we long to hear.
Popcorn stringing? Such a chore!
But laugh we must, and then encore!

Prismatic Sparkle on Soft White

Candy canes hang in a whirl,
As kids dream big, their heads all swirl.
A squirrel darts, what a prank,
While cookies crumble, who will thank?

The stars are bright, like glitter spills,
Snowball fights up on the hills.
A snowman's grin, all carrot flair,
But wait—his nose? Lost in mid-air!

The snowflakes fall like powdered sugar,
Fighting with scarves, oh what a rigger!
Hot cocoa spills, it's a snowy mess,
Yet laughter reigns, we still digress.

With mittens tangled, we stomp and play,
Making snow angels, hip-hip-hooray!
With each silly fall, the fun won't slow,
Our prismatic joy does surely glow!

Celestial Whispers Beneath the Stars

Under twinkling lights we gleam,
While mischief floats like a dream.
A puppy leaps, he snags a hat,
While Santa yells, 'What's up with that?'

The trees adorned in tinsel bright,
A squirrel sneaks in, what a sight!
He swipes a bulb, off it goes,
And crashes down—oh, where it blows!

The sleigh bells jingle, oh so loud,
While elves all prance and play so proud.
But then one trips, right on his feet,
And splashes down—what a cold sheet!

We'll share hot pies, oh what a treat,
With melted marshmallows, quite the feat.
In whispers soft, we'll plan tonight,
With giggles echoing in the light!

A Silver Blanket of Light

The silver sheen blankets our yard,
Where snowmen stand, looking quite hard.
A rabbit hops, loses its way,
Chasing the snowflakes, oh what a play!

The frost on trees, a glittery show,
While children burst with giggles, aglow.
A maple leaf? Oh what a mix,
Brought in by winter, just for kicks!

A cat stalks stealthy on tails of snow,
Only to slide down, 'Whoa, whoa, whoa!'
The jingle bells jangle, a merry cheer,
As winter critters scamper near.

Hot drinks abound, with marshmallows bob,
While rejoicing in the snowy job.
With laughter rich as warm delight,
We'll keep this joy, all through the night!

Whispers of Light in a Winter's Dream

In the night, the snowflakes swirl,
Like tiny dancers in a twirl.
One lands squarely on my nose,
I sneeze, and off the magic goes!

The trees are dressed in frosty gowns,
Like winter queens in snowy towns.
But squirrels steal the twinkling lights,
Now they're hosting wild snowball fights!

Hot cocoa spills on my mittened lap,
Frothy marshmallows take a nap.
I giggle as the snowmen pose,
One's got a carrot for a nose!

So here we laugh under the moon,
While snowflakes play a merry tune.
With each joke that we let go,
Laughter sparkles in the snow!

Flickers of Joy amidst Chilled Serenity

Look at those reindeer in a funk,
Trying to dance but just got drunk.
They tripped and fell upon the ice,
And now they're sliding in a dance so nice!

The stars above are twinkling bright,
But my nose is feeling quite the bite.
With mittens on too big for me,
I'm clapping hands, oh can't you see?

The snowmen laugh, their hats askew,
One spins around—ah, what a view!
They tell me jokes that make me giggle,
Then break apart in one big wiggle!

As we swirl in this chilly blast,
I'm glad I've got a snowball cast!
We'll hurl and shout with all our might,
Creating joy in this winter night!

Moonbeams Playing on a Snowy Palette

Moonlight bathes the world in white,
But I’ve lost my shoe, oh what a sight!
The snowmen chuckle, their eyes aglow,
While I dance barefoot, making snow!

The flakes are falling like soft confetti,
But my feet are cold, and not too ready.
With every step, I slip and slide,
My friends all laugh, their cheeks puffed wide!

Here comes a cat with a winter hat,
Looking regal, how about that?
She prances by, finds snow to pounce,
And suddenly, we’re in a winter bounce!

So let’s all giggle through the frost,
With every moment, we think we’re lost.
Our laughter echoes, sweet and true,
In this winter wonderland, me and you!

Frozen Stars in a Blanket of White

The stars are frozen, or so they say,
As the snowflakes dance and play.
They swirl around, a frosty crew,
While I try to hula-hoop, who knew?

My scarf is tangled, oh what a mess,
But the snowman says, "Just wear it like a dress!"
I chuckle as I make a mound,
While penguins join us, making a sound!

There's a squirrel stealing all the treats,
As I slip on ice, oh, how my heart beats!
But it's all worth it for the fun we share,
In this winter wonderland beyond compare!

With frozen stars brightening the scene,
We’ll laugh together, the happiest team.
From snowball fights to endless cheer,
This winter magic brings us near!

Whisper of the Frozen Stars

In the night where snowflakes prance,
The reindeer stop to take a chance.
They laugh at penguins, dressed in style,
And slide around, oh what a mile!

With frosty breath and jolly cheer,
They spin and twirl without any fear.
A snowman shuffles, slips on ice,
And yells, "Hey, that was really nice!"

The moon just giggles, full and round,
While snowballs fly and laughter's found.
A frozen fork gets stuck in snow,
But no one cares, they steal the show!

So raise a mug with marshmallows,
To frosty friends and silly fellows.
In this winter, full of glee,
Who knew ice could be so free?

Celestial Dance on Icy Veils

Elves waltz under a cold blue sky,
As snowflakes whisper a gentle sigh.
They trip on twinkling lights galore,
And tumble in snow, then laugh and roar!

Snowmen strut with scarves so bright,
While gingerbread men compete in flight.
The cookie crowns a missing nose,
With icing dreams, oh, how it glows!

The sleigh bells jingle without a care,
As raindrops freeze in the frosty air.
A penguin steals a carrot stick,
And laughs, “That’s just my little trick!”

Beneath the glow of lights so high,
Snowflakes dance, and spirits fly.
Who knew winter could be this fun?
A frosty world for everyone!

Ethereal Sparkle in the Air

With every snicker, the snowflakes laugh,
A hopping rabbit splits in half!
He puffs and puffs, then falls, oh dear,
And plops right down in snowy cheer!

The snowman's hat is way too big,
A little girl's beam lights up the fig.
She spins him round until he sways,
And giggles as he melts away!

The stars wink down, stuck in a dance,
While squirrels join in, not missing a chance.
They toss confetti but—uh-oh—look!
It's just the snow from the overhead nook!

So let's toast to this icy fun,
With marshmallow hats, for everyone!
A winter's giggle, bright and gay,
In the frosty chill, we dance and play!

Glistening Tidings of the Heart

With every snowflake that takes its turn,
The kids throw snowballs, oh, how they yearn.
For chilly rounds of silly fights,
And laughter echoes through the nights!

Hot cocoa spills, but who can scold?
It’s a wintery world where dreams unfold.
The snowflakes twinkle, meeting the ground,
As smiles bubble up all around!

In this frosty, sparkly sphere,
A cat in a scarf brings endless cheer.
She prances around, a clumsy sight,
Chasing shadows with all her might!

So here’s to frolics and whimsy galore,
As we dance and sing by the front door.
With giggles and joy all through the night,
This chilly fest surely feels just right!

Glittering Frost Amidst Snowy Silence

The ground is white, it looks so neat,
I slipped and fell right on my seat.
Frosty fingers waving cheer,
Laughing snowflakes, oh so near.

Sneaky flakes, they land on my nose,
Quickly melting, where do they go?
Snowman grins with a carrot spy,
'Tell me more,' he asks with a sigh.

My cat in snow boots, what a sight!
Chasing shadows, oh, what delight.
Snowballs fly, a cheeky throw,
Turns my brother into a snow glow.

Under the moon, we giggle loud,
Making memories, feeling proud.
With frosty fun and silly cheer,
Glittering nights, we hold so dear.

Nightfall Illuminated by Icy Stars

Winter nights, so crisp and clear,
Snowflakes dance, like they're a peer.
A snowman wears sunglasses cool,
Winking at the frosty pool.

Chocolate mugs, we sip and sigh,
As playful pups jump high up, oh my!
A sledge ride goes a little wild,
I swear I heard that reindeer smiled.

Fluffy mittens on hapless hands,
Dropping snowballs, making plans.
Giggles echo, the night grows bright,
Stars join us in pure delight.

Silly hats, we tip and cheer,
To our neighbors, warm with holiday cheer.
We cozy up, let laughter flow,
Under the icy stars' sweet glow.

Sparkling Gleams on a Winter's Night

Sipping cocoa, marshmallows in a row,
Snowflakes tickle, giving a show.
Frosty feet in fluffy socks,
While the snowman confuses the clocks.

A snowball fight, who will prevail?
Oops, I missed, hit a friendly pale!
Dashboard angels, making a scene,
Don't mind the neighbor's grumpy machine.

Around the fire, we share a tale,
Of how snow was born from a whale.
Laughter echoes, filling the night,
As shadows dance in the faint moonlight.

With every giggle, with every cheer,
Winter's magic is drawing near.
So we wrap it up with silly grace,
Sparkling dreams in this merry place.

Veil of Light Over the Snow-Capped Dreams

In the moon's embrace, we find our song,
Snowflakes twirl like dancers all night long.
Chasing rabbits, oh what a spree,
Who knew winter could be this zany?

The snowman wonders, 'Where's my hat?'
As warm winds chuckle at the splat.
A flock of geese starts to glare,
'You call this snow? Please, let us share!'

A graceful deer bounds in tight circles,
Ignoring the antics of eager turtles.
With a wink and a hearty cheer,
We all join in, bringing the cheer!

As we scheme and play under moonlight beams,
Breathless laughter fills our dreams.
With a sprinkle of whimsy and silly delight,
A veil of light on this cheerful night.

A Tapestry of Radiance and White

Twinkling bulbs hang from the eaves,
While snowmen dance in goofy heaves.
Your latte spills as you slip on ice,
At least the snowflakes look really nice.

Kids make angels, flailing around,
While their pets just stare, looking quite wound.
Puppies skitter, chasing their tails,
While mittens wander off on the trails.

Hot cocoa overflows in the mug,
With marshmallows bouncing, oh what a shrug!
Whipped cream birds take flight like a dream,
While laughter tickles the frosty stream.

Cheerful chaos fills the winter air,
As dad wears a hat that's utterly rare.
With our silly hats and our frozen noses,
We embrace the joy that each flake exposes.

Echoes of Light Upon Chilled Earth

Footprints crunch on a snow-sweet path,
While neighbors shiver, trying to laugh.
Scarf wrapped tight, but my nose is red,
I think I need a warm blanket instead.

Snowball fights turn into a catastrophe,
As children dodge like they're on a spree.
A rogue snowbank claims an unsuspecting foot,
Leaving parents with laughter, not a single smoot.

Holiday sweaters, a sight to behold,
With patterns of reindeer and stories retold.
Yet someone forgot to pack the right size,
A perfect fit for a dinner surprise!

With lights aglow, a shimmery show,
Our rooftop icicles, look at them glow!
As neighbors complain of the glowing haze,
We laugh it off through the winter gaze.

The Night Sky's Gift to Silent Streets

Streetlights flicker like fireflies bright,
Illuminating the snow in the night.
Sleds crash into fences in pure delight,
While hot cider spills—oh, what a sight!

Laughter erupts in the chill of the air,
As someone’s scarf gets caught in a bear.
They run with a dash, a flurry, a swirl,
While our cheerful songs make the silence twirl.

Frosty whispers tickle the noses,
As snowflakes tumble like playful dozes.
Even the grumpiest neighbors are caught,
In the holiday spirit—well, somewhat fraught!

Beneath the moon's watchful, glimmering stance,
Families gather for a festive dance.
With feet that slip and hats that fly,
We savor each moment with hearts in the sky.

Frosted Gleams and Heavenly Whispers

Chasing raindrops turn to snowflakes,
And with each tumble, the giggle wakes.
The cat darts out in a fluffy flare,
While grandpa snores in the rocking chair.

Shoveling snow with a shovel that’s broken,
While neighbors gather, sharing the joking.
A snowman appears with a carrot nose,
Right next to three hats, who knows how it grows?

Children's laughter fills the crisp, cool air,
While the squirrels prepare for an acorn affair.
Christmas cookies wink with sneaky intent,
As crumbs vanish, oh what a event!

With lights and sounds dancing in glee,
The magic of winter brings us esprit.
As we toast to the season, our hearts write a tune,
Under the twinkling stars and the watchful moon.

Frozen Glimmers of Nostalgic Whispers

Frosty flakes fall like silly dreams,
Old sweaters dance and rip at seams.
Icicles hang like teeth on show,
Cheerful gnomes, they steal the show.

Hot cocoa spills from mugs in cheer,
But grandma swears it's good this year!
We build a man made of a sock,
Named him 'Frosty'—what a shock!

Snowmen wobble, lose a nose,
I swear they had more style, goodness knows!
But giggles carry through the chill,
As winter starts to give us thrills.

With cheeks aglow and noses red,
We chase the dogs while they chase, instead!
A world of laughter, bright and wide,
In frosty fun, we'll take a ride!

A Winter's Shimmer Beneath the Starlit Sky

The nighttime twinkles, like a wink,
Snowflakes swirl and make us think.
Why does the snowball aim for me?
Did you see that, oh so free?

A snow angel's face looks quite bizarre,
Did someone tell her she's a star?
Falling flat with a joyful thud,
Squeaks and laughs erupt like flood.

Sleds are racing down the hill,
The brave ones scream with major thrill.
With each tumble and silly flip,
Who knew fun could be such a trip?

And snowmen gather to take a bow,
As carrots march while we laugh loud.
With hot cocoa, we toast the night,
In winter's charm, there's pure delight!

Harmony of Light on Snowy Silence

At twilight’s glance, the snow looks pink,
The pancakes ferociously make us stink.
But fluffy treats in mouths will intersect,
While outside cold makes our cheeks reflect.

The snowball fights don’t play it nice,
Caught my friend unaware—oh, what a slice!
With giggles ringing through the air,
A mound of snow, our laughter's flair.

Sleds go flying down the slope,
With plenty of cheers, and none of hope.
As feet slip out from underneath,
We tumble, chin to snow—no grief!

The night sky dances on the white,
Our frosty antics bring delight.
Wraps and giggles through the cold,
In this chilly chaos, joy unfolds!

Elysian Frost and Celestial Tranquility

Oh frosty nights bring merry sights,
With bunnies dancing in snowy tights.
We'll charm our friends with antics fun,
Creating laughter, a race to run.

With snowflakes tickling on our nose,
We chase each other, giggles expose.
A snowball glances off with a splat,
Until we all just wear a flat!

Grandma's pie burns in the night,
We claim it's "charred"—oh, what a plight!
But with warm hearts and happy cries,
Even burnt crust can win the prize.

As winter whispers all around,
In cheerful shouts, true joy is found.
So raise your mugs, let's cheer once more,
For frosty fun we all adore!

Traces of Light Across a Wintry Canvas

In a town where snowballs glide,
Chubby snowmen sleep and slide.
I saw a squirrel wearing a hat,
He looked quite dapper, imagine that!

Footprints dance and shuffle near,
Snowflakes giggle, oh what cheer!
They tickle noses, make us sneeze,
While penguins host a snowball tease.

Ducks with scarves waddle about,
Conducting carols loud and stout.
A sleigh gets stuck in piles of fluff,
The reindeer say, “That’s quite enough!”

Hot cocoa spills, a marshmallow's flight,
A caffeine comet, oh what a sight!
As snow angels wave their frosty hands,
We melt with laughter, in snowy lands.

Sparkling Night Memories in the Snow

Twinkling lights on frosted trees,
A raccoon dances with such ease.
He boots it up in snowflake shoes,
While kids throw snow, truce to amuse!

Elves in pajamas, quite a sight,
Sneak cookies from the pantry tonight.
Frosty with a carrot nose,
Is plotting mischief, goodness knows!

A cat in boots, a hat askew,
Chasing snowflakes, just for you.
Neighbors laugh, their cheeks aglow,
As winter chuckles in the snow.

Gifts wrapped tight, what's inside?
A rubber chicken? What a ride!
With silent nights and you can bet,
These memories, we won't forget!

Enchanted Crystal Tales in Wintry Nights

Under the moon with icy grace,
Snowflakes twirl, a wild race.
A dog in boots leaps with joy,
Chasing shadows like a toy!

A flurry of giggles, reindeer prance,
While snowmen break out in dance.
With carrot noses all askew,
They laugh and say, “How do you do?”

Elves on board, a sledding spree,
Telling tales of cups of tea.
They spill secrets, ‘round the fire,
As marshmallow fluff climbs higher and higher!

With twinkling stars and frosty trails,
The snowman sings, his voice prevails.
In this wonder, joy bestowed,
Humor flourishes, winter glowed.

Stars' Chorus Over a Winter Landscape

The night is bright, with giggles here,
As penguins juggle, full of cheer.
Snowflakes whisper, shining bright,
Like tiny dancers, pure delight.

Frogs in hats, they croak a tune,
Underneath a winking moon.
While snowplows chase a rooftop cat,
He yells, “No fair!” How about that?

With winter fruits that slip and slide,
Kids dive in, at sheer joy they ride.
A cereal snowman, quite absurd,
Wishes for pancakes, it’s unheard!

Meanwhile, the stars, they start to sing,
“Come one, come all, to winter’s fling!”
A tapestry of laughter spun,
In this wonderland, we all are one.

Milton Keynes UK
Ingram Content Group UK Ltd.
UKHW022340171124
451242UK00007B/70

9 789916 941140